NO EASY DAYS

*The Incredible Drama
of Naval Aviation*

NO
EASY
DAYS

*The Incredible Drama
of Naval Aviation*

Douglas Keeney
William Butler

BKF

This book was inspired by the very popular
home video series, *The Challenge of Flight*.
We tip our hat to its creator and our friend, Don Farmer.

Thanks also to Jeff Ethell for his invaluable assistance.

ISBN 1-884532-15-2

Photos courtesy of The Department of Defense Still Media Records Center,
The National Archives and Records Administration, and the Naval Safety Center.

Printed in Canada

Published by Butler+Keeney+Farmer
3900 Shelbyville Road
Louisville, Kentucky 40207
502•895•3939

(Preceding page) An F4U Corsair gets waved off the USS *Wasp*.
P-factor torque will invert the aircraft, and it will crash into the water.

N aval aviation is the most demanding flight environment in the world. Most pilots wouldn't even consider doing what a naval aviator does, much less do it day in and day out.

It's not enough, after all, that the runways are a fraction of the length of a land-based runway or that the decks are cold, slippery steel. Nor is it enough that the boat is steaming away from you while you land (and as you do, your wingtips are mere feet from the carrier's island). No. On top of it all, the entire ship's crew is watching you, and your landing will be graded. Formally. For the records. No matter what your rank.

All this has to do with one point: You must be carrier qualified. You must maintain that qualification. And you'd better be good at it.

Carrier aviation is not the same as flying in the Air Force. And not in just the obvious ways, either. Yes, the decks are small and the swirl of jets and props is dangerous and almost unreal, but the differences are in the little things, too. For instance, during World War II, the F4U Corsair, one of the Marine's finest fighters, was almost unsuitable for carrier operations. Why? The airplane tended to bounce when

The F-14 Tomcat in full afterburner.

INTRODUCTION

8

(Left) An F4U Corsair in flames after a deck impact on the USS Sicily. *Note that the left underwing pylon is empty. The pylons are designed to carry either 1000 pound bombs or 154 gallon drop tanks.*

(Below) This F/A-18 Hornet bursts into flames during takeoff from MCAS Twenty-Nine Palms (California). The pilot ejected successfully but the aircraft was lost. The Hornet is struck during the most critical phase of the takeoff—just moments after the mains clear the runway and while the jet is in full afterburner. An improperly secured fuel cap was the cause of this mishap.

it landed. That's OK for a land-based fighter with a long runway ahead of it, but bounce on the carrier deck and you might skip the arrestor cables and perhaps plow into the barrier. Or worse.

Or this. Years later, the S-3's acceptance into the fleet was delayed because the Viking was such an aerodynamically clean airplane. A clean aircraft usually means a faster, more fuel-efficient aircraft, both highly desirable characteristics in a military jet. In naval carrier terms, it also means a jet that can get in the groove and hold the glideslope with engine power way low in the rpm's. The groove is the final quarter mile or so behind the ship, and if you needed quick power, engines low in the rpm's are unresponsive. An unwitting naval aviator might push the throttles forward expecting a response only to find none and then smash into the ramp.

No, the Navy does not easily let people or airplanes on the carrier. Consider the F9F Panther. The Navy modified the jet into what would be called the dash-5 version but they were not about to accept it until they tested it. You might think the photo sequence on pages 102-105 represents an example of poor piloting, but in fact the Panther's pilot that day was a highly experienced naval test pilot. Unfortunately, the dash-5 hit the burble behind the carrier and failed to power up through it. Incredibly, the pilot survived and was back flying in six months.

The "burble", of course, is another nuance of carrier aviation. When you push a 90,000 ton aircraft carrier across the surface of the sea, the hull splits up the air in all sorts of angles and the island disrupts the flow down the flight deck. The resulting mishmash of currents gathers up behind the ship's stern — directly in the path of a landing aircraft. That mass of air is the burble.

Just how bad the burble will be one day to the next is entirely unpredictable.

Each and every phase of carrier flight operations has been tested and re-tested, again and again, and yet there are mishaps. Some are easy to understand — like the bounce in the F4U's landings or the a AD Skyraider's propensity to trip on the barrier, while others are more complex, like the S-3 Viking's almost invisible pitfall.

This Navy A-7 Corsair winds up in an unusual place after a training mishap. Salvage operations will begin after this crew figures out the best way to handle the wreckage. The A-7 was retired by the Navy just after the Gulf War.

An SH-2F Seasprite is pulled out of San Diego Harbor during salvage operations. The helo was assigned to fleet anti-submarine duty.

This SH-2H suffered an engine failure while on a routine anti-submarine patrol in the Indian Ocean. Operating from the USS Kitty Hawk, one skiff is returning the helo's survivors to the carrier while a second skiff carries crash investigators around the sinking wreckage. The camera angle and the diffusion caused by the covering sea water give the Seasprite a whale-like appearance.

Nonetheless, each mishap that has been photographed leaves an oddly interesting visual record. Look at the AF-2S on page 63. Or the striking composition on the cover.

The mishaps in this book were gathered from the photographic records of the National Archives, the Pentagon's Still Media Records Center, and the Navy's Flight Safety Center. They cover the last fifty years of carrier flight but they concentrate on the period immediately before and after the Korean conflict. Many include the old straight-decked carriers, while others bridge the last of the World War II aircraft and the first fighters of the Vietnam period.

Photographic records of mishaps are hard to come by. Naturally mishaps are photographed only when a camera is near, which is generally only when the mishap happens on the carrier. Moreover, the Navy today relies almost entirely on videotape and far less on film or still photos. Video tape does not easily — or clearly — convert to still photos, which further reduces the availability of printable records.

(Pages 12-13) This F9F Panther turns sea water into steam as it struggles to gain altitude after a failed barricaded arrestment. The pilot was rescued.

A TBM Avenger rips through the arresting wires, losing its landing gear. During WWII, this aircraft saw extensive duty in the Pacific.

An AD Skyraider has come to rest short of the island after impacting a gun turret on landing. The wing separated at the wing root. The AD's wingspan was actually one of the Navy's widest—50 feet.

Nonetheless, the collection contained herein clearly captures the tremendous obstacles facing the brave men and women who chose carrier aviation. Nothing is easy about flying from a ship. Just why that is true is amply illustrated in the following pages.

And what is the message here? Yes, it is true that every mishap is a lesson learned, and much good is done from the study of these photographs. But there is something larger to be gained from the study of this book. The aftermath of a mishap is time for reflection. In the reading of this pictorial essay it is not inappropriate to pause and reflect on the great privilege we enjoy in large part because of good people willing to live with extreme risks so that we may live in the comfort of peace.

That is a good use of this book.

(Below and right) An F4U Corsair bursts into flames upon landing aboard the USS Coral Sea. *Despite the ensuing fire, the pilot escapes without injury. As soon as the fire is extinguished, it is pushed over the side, a common practice for aircraft that cannot be repaired at sea.*

(Right) Neatly severed forward of the tail section is this F6F Hellcat. A brilliant fighting career during WWII earned this model the respect of the pilots that flew her—and over 5,000 enemy kills. In this 1951 mishap aboard the USS Princeton, a fuselage failure has occurred during arrestment. Note that the tailhook has engaged a wire.

An AD Skyraider loses power on takeoff from the USS Boxer, July 1953. The pilot was uninjured.

MISHAPS

There is an adage in aviation about spins. A spin occurs when the wings lose lift and the aircraft begins to yaw, or spin. The adage goes like this: you can predict the conditions that will start a spin, but you never know how they will develop. One turn or ten, ten thousand feet to pullout or twice that. You just don't know, at least not until it's over.

A corollary to that adage seems to apply to carrier mishaps. You just can't believe all the ways a flight can go wrong. Which is true. There seem to be more ways for an airplane to end up in the drink, smash into the island, or burn on the flight deck than anyone could possibly imagine.

But the fact of the matter is that across the incredible range of mishaps you will see in this section, most were survived without injury. Someone, somewhere did imagine all the ways a flight could go wrong, and wrote the manual that trained the pilots to handle the problem. The results speak for themselves.

(Right) The crew of this helo demonstrates that there is more than one way to get back on deck.

An S3 Viking takes the barricade.

(Preceding pages) Somewhat disorienting is this photograph of an AD Skyraider moments before it impacts the sea, completely inverted.

Enemy anti-aircraft fire damaged this AD Skyraider during
air strikes over Korea, December 1950.

This crash is so violent that the engine has been torn off its mounts.
Despite the fireball, the pilot pushed free of the aircraft.

(Opposite page and right) A Grumman AF-2S Guardian sub killer lost power on takeoff from the USS Bunker Hill *(CVE-106) and was forced to ditch. The injured pilot escaped the sinking aircraft, but his rescue was complicated by tangled shroud lines. After attempts to lift him by helo, he was finally cut free and pulled aboard a whaler dispatched from a nearby destroyer.*

This Douglas AD Skyraider has suffered a violent prop strike—the engine stopped in less than a full rotation. Two blades have completely separated, the third has snapped, and the fourth, while bent, has little damage due to engine rotation. The tailhook is engaged, suggestng that the Skyraider caught a wire in a nose-high attitude.

The Skyraider enjoyed 22 years of service in the U.S. Navy, including duty in Korea and Vietnam. Powered by a 2,500 hp Wright engine, a single AD could carry 8000 pounds of ordnance.

28

This F4U Corsair from the USS Philippine Sea *(CV-47) is ditching into relatively calm seas.*

Unexpectedly, the aircraft noses over rapidly as it impacts the water alongside the carrier.

(Opposite page and above) Blimps—or in Navy parlance, "less-than-rigid airships"—have intrigued military planners since their early use in World War One. Largely, the varied attempts to deploy these airships all ended in the same way—with a crash. In 1952, this Navy blimp was engaged in carrier qualification training on the USS Kula Gulf when it suffered a complete structural failure and collapsed into the sea. The puff of black smoke is from the engine fire that resulted from the impact. The fire extinguished itself as the blimp sank. (Continued on next page)

(Above and right) The USS Bauer, *which was acting as plane guard during the operation, steamed toward the stricken ship, and eventually picked up some of the surviving crew. The submarine USS* Seadog *circled in from the other side, picking up more survivors, but too late to save the airship, which sank 55 miles off the coast of Georgia.*

March 1953: An F9F-4 Panther overshoots the arresting wires aboard the
USS Bennington, *then plunges into the carrier elevator. The Panther was one of Grumman's most*
successful designs. It had a max speed of 575 mph and carried four 20mm cannons in its nose.

The Panther falls on another Panther ready to come up to the flight deck.
Firefighters quickly prevent a major fire, then sort out the ensuing mess.
The Panther was America's first jet to see combat.

(Opposite page and below) Space is at a premium on a carrier. To maximize it, aircraft parked on the flight deck hang over the side of the ship. In 1984, the USS Midway *collided with a Panamanian freighter, the* Cactus. *Both ships suffered extensive damage. Unfortunately, so did three F-4 Phantom II jets. Each of the aircraft lost portions of their tail sections. (Bottom right) The optical landing system platform on the* Midway *is mangled by the force of the collision.*

(Pages 38-39) Carrier decks are slippery, and when the brakes fail, the chances of going over the side are very real. Unhurt, the pilot of this F2H-2 climbs free and is rescued as he floats alongside his carrier, the USS Essex (CV-9).

The McDonnell F2H-2 Banshee was the Navy's second carrier jet (the first was its older brother, the F1H), and entered service in 1947. It made history when a pilot made the first U.S. ejection from an aircraft (a successful one, at that). The Banshee had a top speed of 532 mph.

An unusual mishap involving this A-6 Intruder made for a particularly odd photograph. While comfortably cruising at 8000 feet and at 230 knots, the BN's ejection seat suddenly fired, but only partially. The BN went through the canopy, then stopped, half in and half out. The pilot immediately slowed the Intruder and descended to the carrier. He made a one-wire pass. Incredibly, the BN suffered only a separated shoulder. The pilot received the Air Medal for his actions.

Notice the BN's parachute wrapped around the tail. This actually prevented the right seater from crashing forward into the jagged canopy glass as the A-6 trapped.

LOSS OF POWER

A Navy fighter is launched from the carrier deck by a steam catapult. Like any jet, Navy jets are susceptible to sudden engine fires or power losses. (In fact, Navy jets have perhaps an even higher risk of loss-of-power. They must be tested to handle the big gulp of steam they will surely swallow at the end of the cat stroke.)

Unlike Air Force jets, though, Navy jets have no runway for a takeoff abort. If a Navy jet loses power on takeoff, there are just sixty feet of gravy to play with before the jet will impact the sea. If the plane does go into the drink, it is vitally important to remember the large aircraft carrier bearing down on you—you can be sure it won't stop on a dime—and the tendency for fighters to sink quickly.

(Above and right) The AF-2S Guardian carried a lot of aircraft behind its single 2800 hp Pratt & Whitney engine. A sudden loss of power during takeoff was survived by its crew. The radar operator is seen emerging from his fuselage hatch.

The Guardian, fitted with the lower radome, was the leading element in the Navy's anti-submarine hunter-killer force.

(Preceding pages) An F9F loses power on takeoff.

A loss of power can lead to a stall which, in turn, often leads to a spin. This F4U Corsair has launched off the USS Bon Homme Richard *and is clearly entering the stall. The pronounced nose-down attitude and the ensuing splash indicate that a controlled crash was unlikely. Note the nonchalance of the sailor in the foreground.*

The F4U had a dangerous left-wing-down tendency in the stall. Strips were added to induce even stalling between the wings, but the Corsair never became docile. During WWII, the Corsair struggled to gain carrier qualification despite its greater popularity with the land-based Marines who flew her. The Vought F4U production line was reopened during the Korean War. This loss-of-power took place on the USS Philippine Sea.

(Pages 48-49) This AD Skyraider has suffered intermittent engine failure during the takeoff roll. It strikes the 5" gun turret and veers off the side of the USS Leyte (CV-32). Getting the airplane's wings level, the pilot successfully ditches and can be seen egressing from the sinking aircraft.

The pilot of this F4U Corsair impacts the sea wing-down, and with force enough to explode. Nevertheless, he soon bobs free from the wreckage and is rescued within one minute of splash-down.

In this sequence of photographs, the pilot of an AD suffers an engine failure on takeoff and impacts the sea at gross takeoff weight. The force of the crash injures his back and partially paralyzes his legs. Through sheer effort, he finally gets free of the aircraft just moments before it sinks.

(Pages 52-53) Despite twin Westing-house turbojet engines, loss-of-power spelled disaster for this F2H Banshee. Notice that the left wing tank has been left behind on the flight deck.

WAVE-OFFS

In a Navy tactical fighter, there is no such thing as a copilot. The backseater has a job, but it doesn't include flying the jet. That's the pilot's job. The pilot makes the choices, the decisions are his and his alone.

Not so when coming aboard the ship. Snugly in the groove, the pilot flies the aircraft in concert with the Landing Signal Office—the LSO. If the LSO likes what he sees, the pilot will receive a signal—the cut—and he is cleared to land. If the LSO doesn't like what he sees, one of four advisories will follow—power, lineup, attitude, or waveoff. If the LSO still doesn't like the approach, he will order the pilot to make the corrections. If the approach continues to look bad, the LSO will wave the jet off and send it around for another pass.

There are four outcomes to any approach, and only one is ideal—a landing, called a trap. The other three—a bolter, a waveoff, or a crash—are terribly poor substitutes. If a pilot suffers too many bolters or waveoffs, the pressure intensifies and the

(Pages 56-57) Interesting detail can be seen in this go-around mishap on the USS Tarawa. *On landing, the Bearcat bounces back into the air and turns toward the island. Yanking the F8F around the island costs the fighter its last lift, and it crashes into the sea. The pilot stands out clearly as he passes the island and again as he surfaces beside his sinking airplane.*

(Preceding pages) An AD Skyraider veers left during an unsuccessful waveoff.

pilot's confidence erodes. A crash, of course, speaks for itself.

LSOs are experienced carrier pilots standing on the edge of the deck watching and advising the landing aircraft. Their eyes are incredible instruments. While they are positioned well away from the landing area, a good deal of risk, nonetheless, goes with the LSO's job. With just seconds in the balance, the LSO on page 96 correctly calculates the point of impact for an F7U sure to crash — and dashes across the flight deck to safety.

His platform is cinderized.

(Opposite page and above) Out-of-control and low over the carrier deck is an almost unmanageable situation. This TBM strikes the flight deck left wing down and careens over the side of the USS Tarawa.

(Pages 60-61) The radome snaps off an F9F Panther as it porpoises down the flight deck of the USS Bon Homme Richard. *The wild ride ends in the sea during these exercises off the coast of San Diego.*

(Pages 62-63) This unfortunate bolter involving an AF-2S Guardian progresses into a spectacular out-of-control that ends in a most unusual position. The radar operator seems to egress first.

Jet engines are slower to spool up to power than are piston engines, making underpowered approaches and low ball waveoffs hard to overcome. This F2H-3 Banshee remains on the edge of the deck after a landing deck-strike. The pilot wound up in the water, but was rescued by helo and returned to the flight deck of his carrier, the USS Bennington *(CVA-20).*

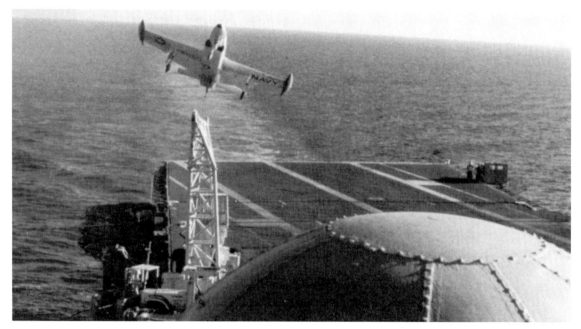

A low-ball waveoff ends in tragedy for this T2 flying carrier quals from the USS Lexington. *The aircraft inverts and crashes into the island. The pilot ejected upside down over the carrier deck.*

(Pages 66-67) The North American AJ-2 Savage provided the Navy with a nuclear strike aircraft, but it ultimately proved to be too large for extensive carrier operations. Its mission was gradually replaced by jets. It was a useful plane, however, and some Savages were converted to aerial reconnaissance, others to aerial refueling. Here, a broken tailhook turns an ordinary trap into an agonizingly slow out-of-control into the sea. There were no injuries. From the USS Yorktown.

(Pages 68-69) The tailhook drags behind an F9F attempting to trap aboard the USS Philippine Sea *(CVA-47). The pilot was beyond the waveoff and was unable to bolter.*

As deck crewmen scramble out of the way of the careening F9F, the landing Panther strikes two other Panthers waiting to launch from the forward cats. He comes to rest on the edge of the deck.

An AD Skyraider loses power on a routine go-around above the USS Leyte, *striking another AD on the deck.*

An incredulous pilot sits dazed in his all-but-destroyed Skyraider as damage control rushes in with the hoses.

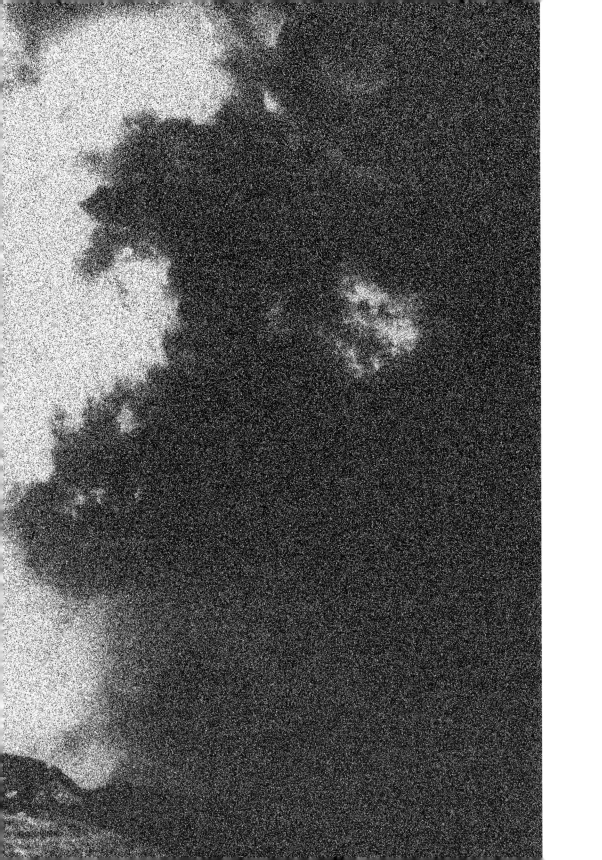

BARRIERS

On today's angled deck carriers, there are four sets of wires traversing the aft portion of the flight deck. Most naval aviators will never use anything more than those cables to land. That is called a trap. A good trap is called an OK three wire—the aviator caught the third wire forward from the stern.

On the old straight deck carriers, there were a great many more wires crossing the deck—eight or nine. Most aviators trapped in those wires.

The few that bounced hard or complicated their landing with too much speed or altitude and failed to waveoff would be arrested in the barriers. At least three barriers protected the rest of the carrier from such pilots.

On today's carriers the angled deck itself protects the carrier from all but the most disastrous landings. There are circumstances, however, for the barricade. The barricade is pulled up when a crippled aircraft is inbound. For these airplanes the high net, while intimidating, is a blessing. Without it, or a shore divert, they would have to eject alongside the ship.

Although necessary, the older barriers caused many problems of their own, as the following photos illustrate.

(Preceding pages) When a 12,000 pound jet goes out of control on a carrier deck, the problems quickly build. A sailor is silhouetted by the flames from the crash of an F2H Banshee. The Banshee took the barricade but it failed, and the jet smashed into other fueled Banshees on the forward end of the flight deck.

(Pages 74-75) An A-7 Corsair takes the barricade and successfully recovers despite a snapped nose wheel and a hung bomb.

*Despite an abundance of wires traversing the flight deck,
each elevated by bowed, flat springs of steel, hooks do fail
to engage. This AD has floated above the cables and is
tripped up by the barrier.*

This Bearcat trips over the barrier wire and flips first on its nose, then over on its back. Flames are quickly extinguished by the fire crew. The vertical stabilizer protects the canopy—and its occupant—with just inches to spare.

(Pages 78-79) This F8F Bearcat is tripped up by the wires of the barrier. No fewer than fourteen crewmen come to the pilot's rescue.

(Pages 80-81) Veering to the right, this Bearcat impacts the island on the USS Tarawa.

(Pages 82-83) The arresting wires of the USS Tarawa *catch the struts of this AD, pitching it violently forward. Leaking jet fuel ignites and races toward the Skyraider. The pilot climbs to safety with the help of fire-suited rescuers.*

(Pages 84-85) The barrier is effective against virtually any aircraft that it engages. It is of no use, however, to aircraft that float over it. This F4U flies over the barrier, then neatly slices the tail off another Corsair before sailing off the side of the USS Princeton

(Pages 86-87) A failed barricade causes this mishap on the USS Mid-way. *The F9F's tailhook skips all of the wires. The barrier engages the jet, but it breaks. The Panther then slams into other jets parked on the forward section of the flight deck. Three aircraft are carried overboard by the collision.*

(Pages 88-89) Five Grumman Guardians are involved in this mishap. The tailhook has slapped the ramp and has broken. The AF-3S then bounces and sails over the barrier and crashes into four other Guardians on the forward section of the deck. Crash crews respond immediately.

(Pages 90-91) Three Bearcats await takeoff, their props spinning, as a fourth sails toward them over the barrier. As can be seen from the reverse-angle photo at right, the T-100 impacts in between the first two Bearcats in line. Remarkably, there was no fire.

RAMP STRIKES

All crashes are bad. One is not worse than the other. Death, when it occurs, is final whatever the cause. But a ramp strike is what naval aviators fear the most.

A ramp strike means that an aircraft has hit the leading edge of the carrier's flight deck, a part of the deck called the round-down. It is a devastating crash, threatening to the entire flight deck crew. For the aircraft involved, it is like a stick of butter hitting a hot knife.

Naval flight operating procedures call for ten to fifteen feet of clearance between the hook and the deck when crossing the fantail. The tailhook will engage the cables another 200-300 feet down the deck. There is no need to fly a low approach.

Unfortunately, the safe clearance margins are easily lost. Poor power management is often the culprit. The result? A hook slap, which is bad, but OK.

Or a ramp strike, which is nearly always fatal.

(Right) A crash, salvage, and rescue team races toward the A-7 ramp strike, some riding in the P-16 shipboard fire-fighting and rescue truck.

The A-7 Corsair at the moment of impact.

(Preceding pages) Billowing smoke and flames mark the ramp strike of an F2H Banshee. Incredibly, the pilot survived.

The LSO seeks safety and runs across the inbound path of an F7U-3 Cutlass about to strike the ramp on the USS Hancock.

The LSO escapes as the Cutlass bursts into flames on impact. The jet has drifted so far to the left that it actually impacts in front of the LSO's platform.

This 1984 ramp strike involved an A-7E Corsair attempting to recover on the USS Midway (CV-41). The fireball characterizes the extreme violence of a ramp strike. Note the engines as they separate and thrust into the air. The Corsair traveled across the flight deck and over the side of the ship.

The only remaining evidence of the crash is charred debris and a scorched flight deck. The three F4 Phantom IIs seem to be unharmed.

*(Pages 100-101) This rare sequence of photographs captures
the ramp strike of an SB2C Helldiver against the wooden deck
of the USS* Shangri La. *Much of the sturdy Curtiss aircraft
actually ends up on the deck, although there is little forward
momentum after the nose slaps down. The pilot was unhurt.*

On April 8, 1952, during landing exercises, an F9F-5 Panther from the USS Bon Homme Richard *sinks in the burble and strikes the ramp. Cameras on the port side of the flight deck just forward of the barriers catch the initial impact.*

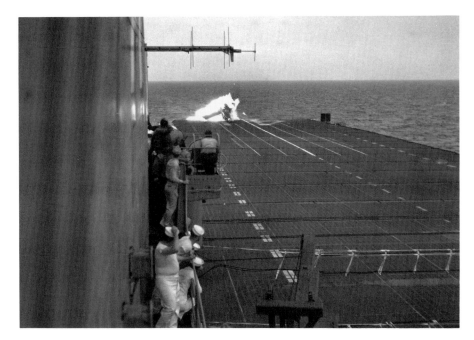 

The jet fuel ignites instantly and rolls down
the flight deck behind the burning canopy.
This crash was captured by both motion
picture and high-speed still cameras. The
motion picture version of this crash has been
incorporated into several Hollywood movies.
(Continued on next page)

*An almost painful detail: the cameras track
the Panther's cockpit as it tumbles down the
flight deck toward the barriers.*

A rescue team member in his fire-retardant suit springs into action and pulls the pilot free from the canopy. The pilot will return to flight status and fly again for the Navy.

(Pages 106-107) An F2H Banshee
makes a futile attempt to clear the
edge of the deck on the USS Oris.
Miraculously, the pilot survived
without injury and continued to fly for
the Navy. Notice the left engine as it
accelerates down the flight deck.

Naval aviation is geared to get its aviators
back on the ship one way or the other, with
their egos bruised and their flight suits wet,
but glad to be alive. The final moments of a
recovery may be quiet, may be humble—
and may be like these.

RECOVERIES